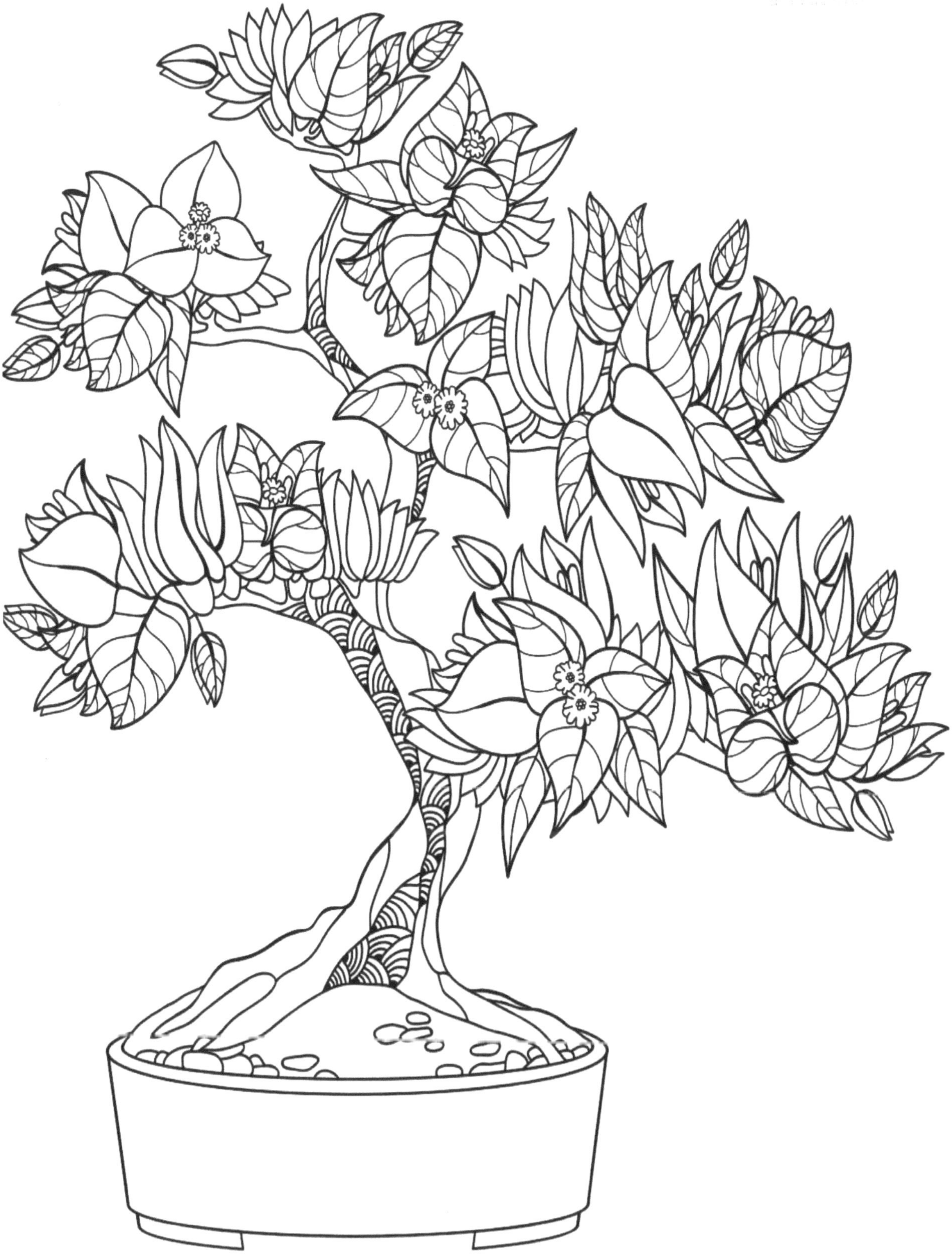

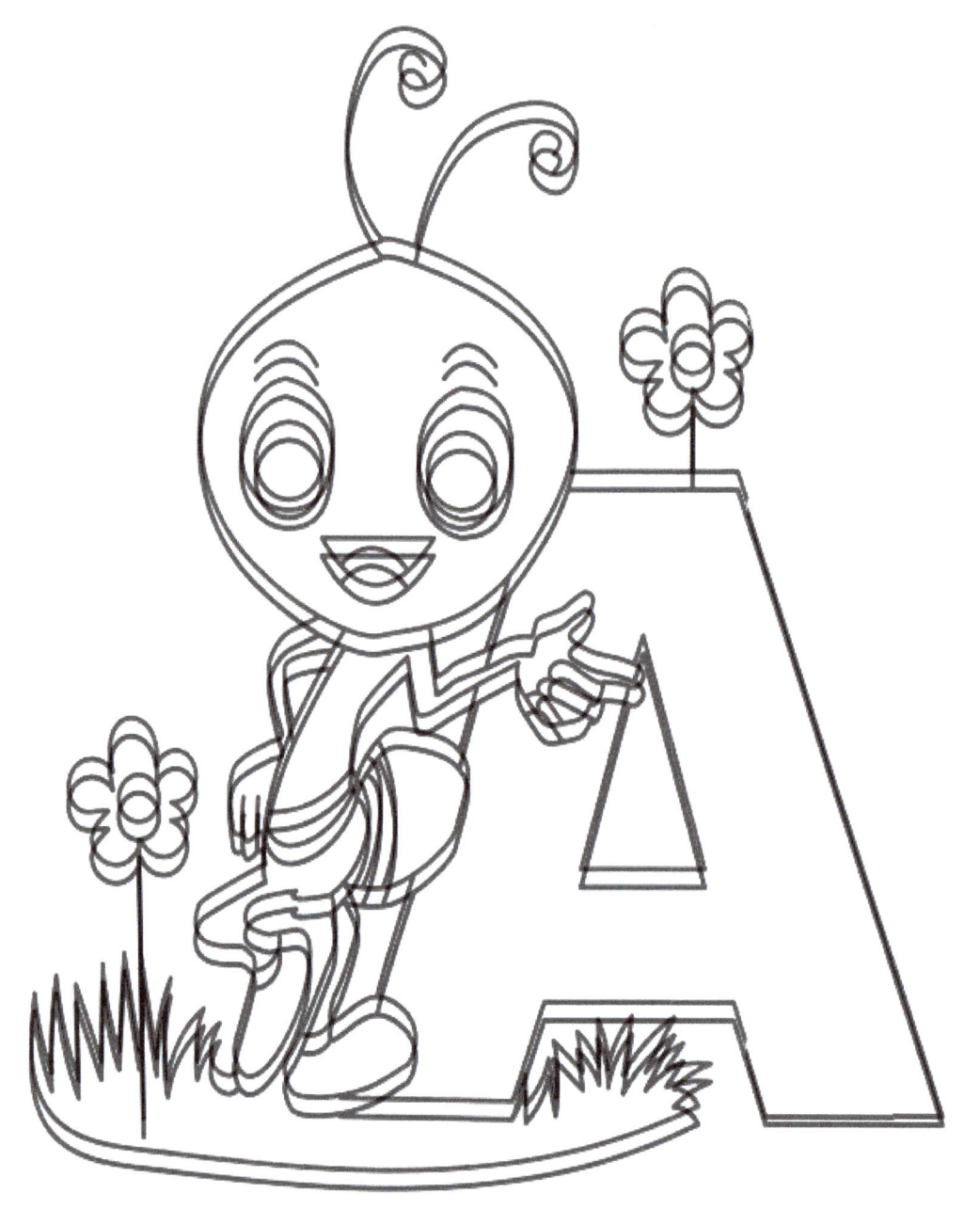

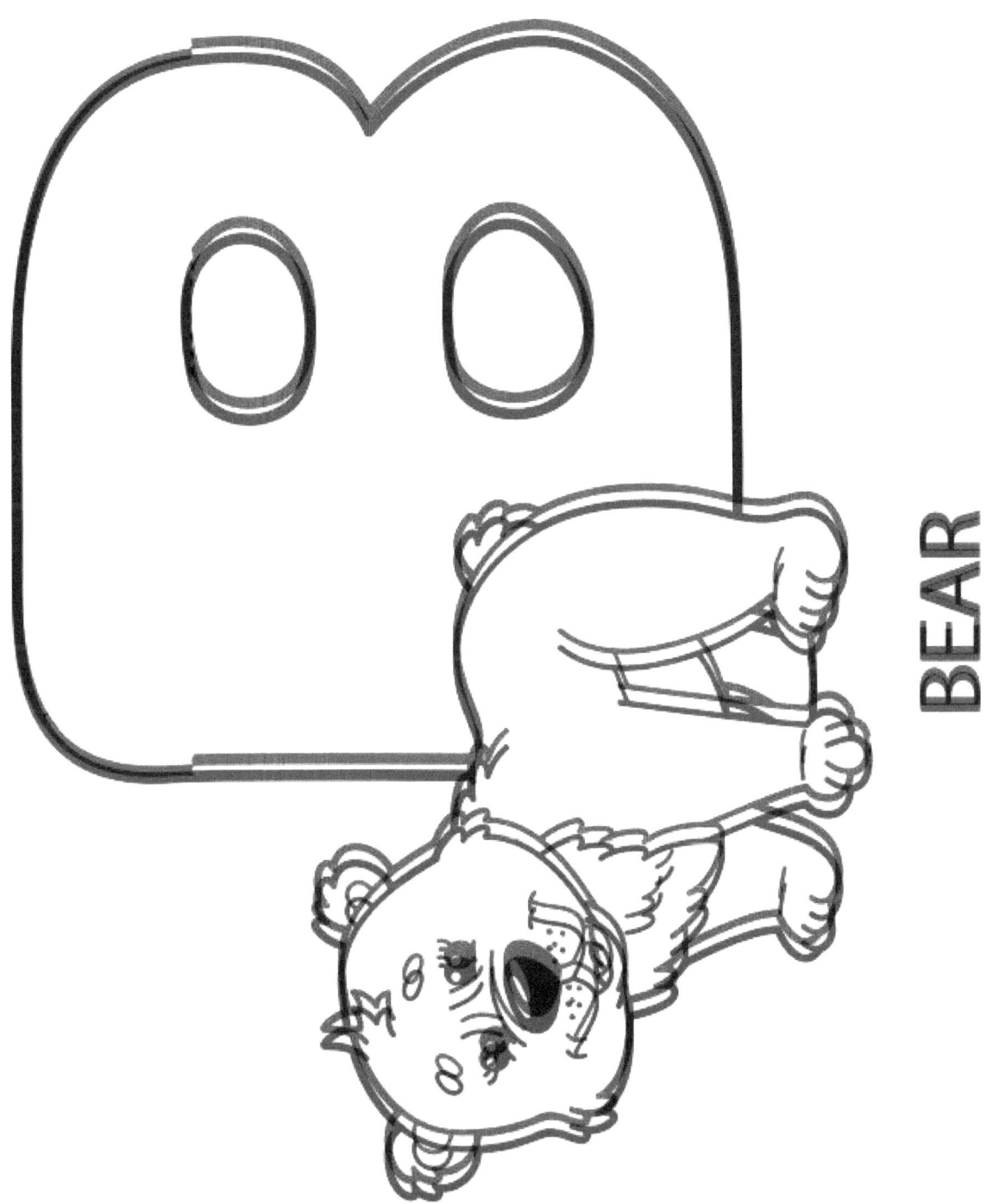

BEAR

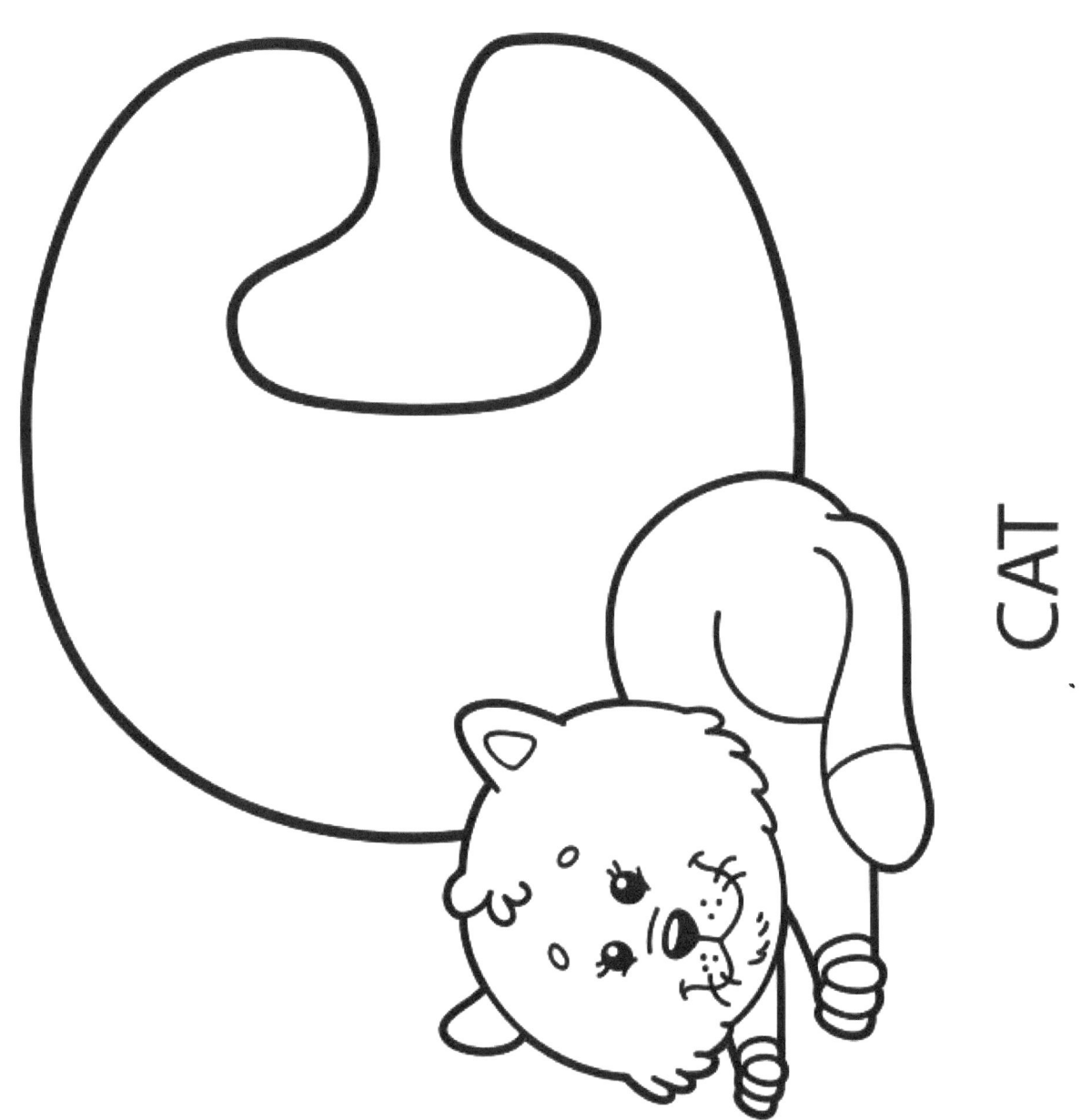

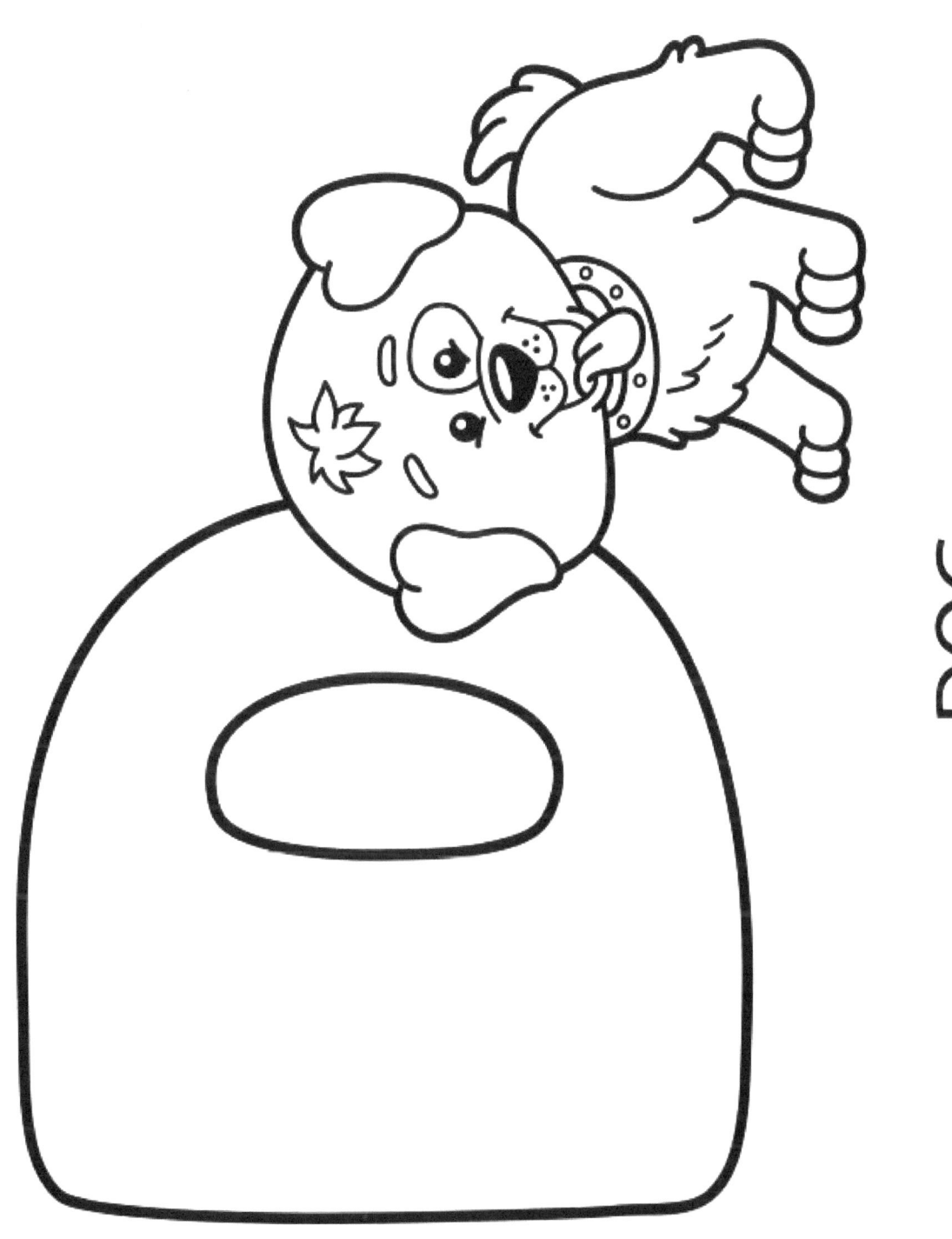

DOG

ELEPHANT

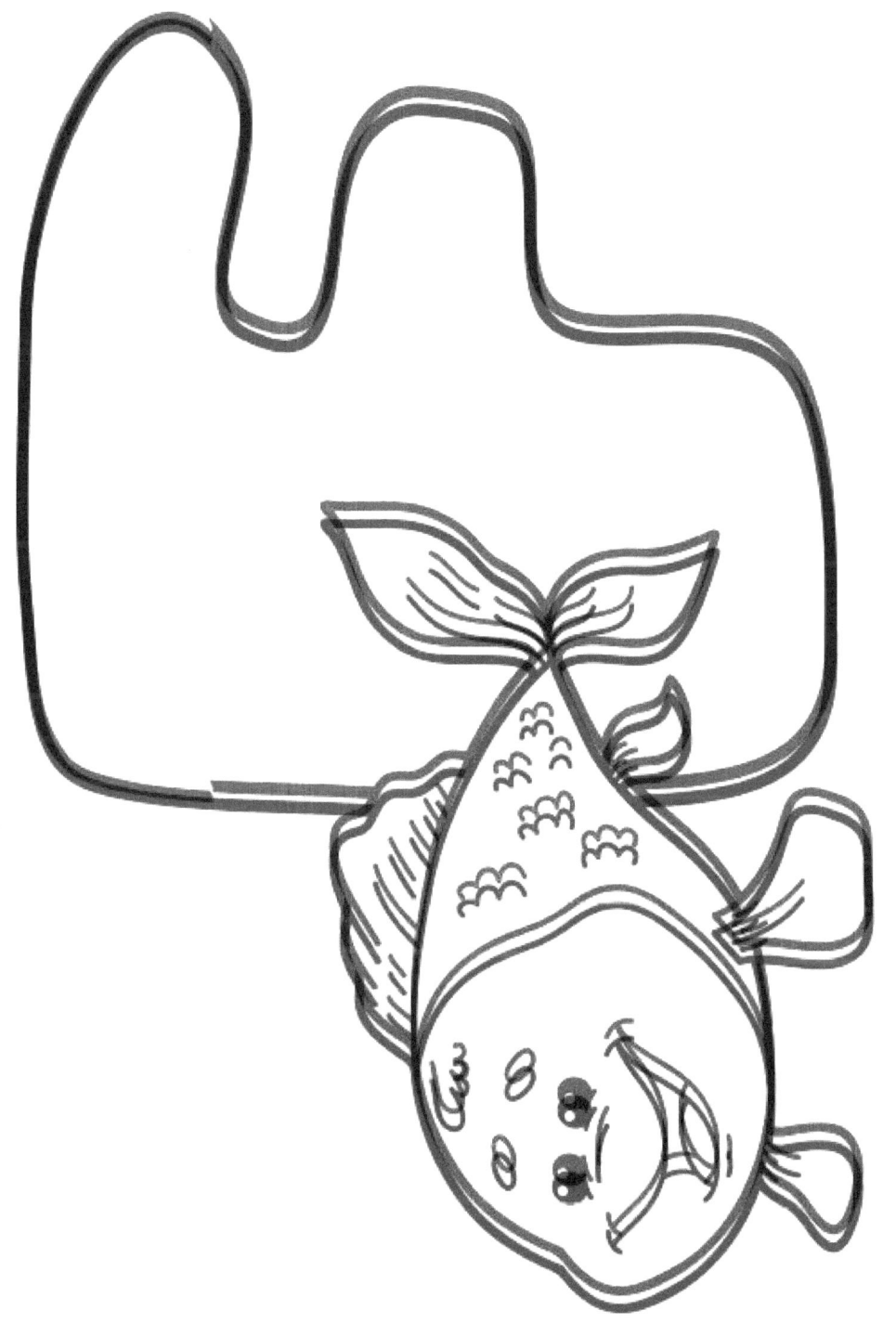

FISH

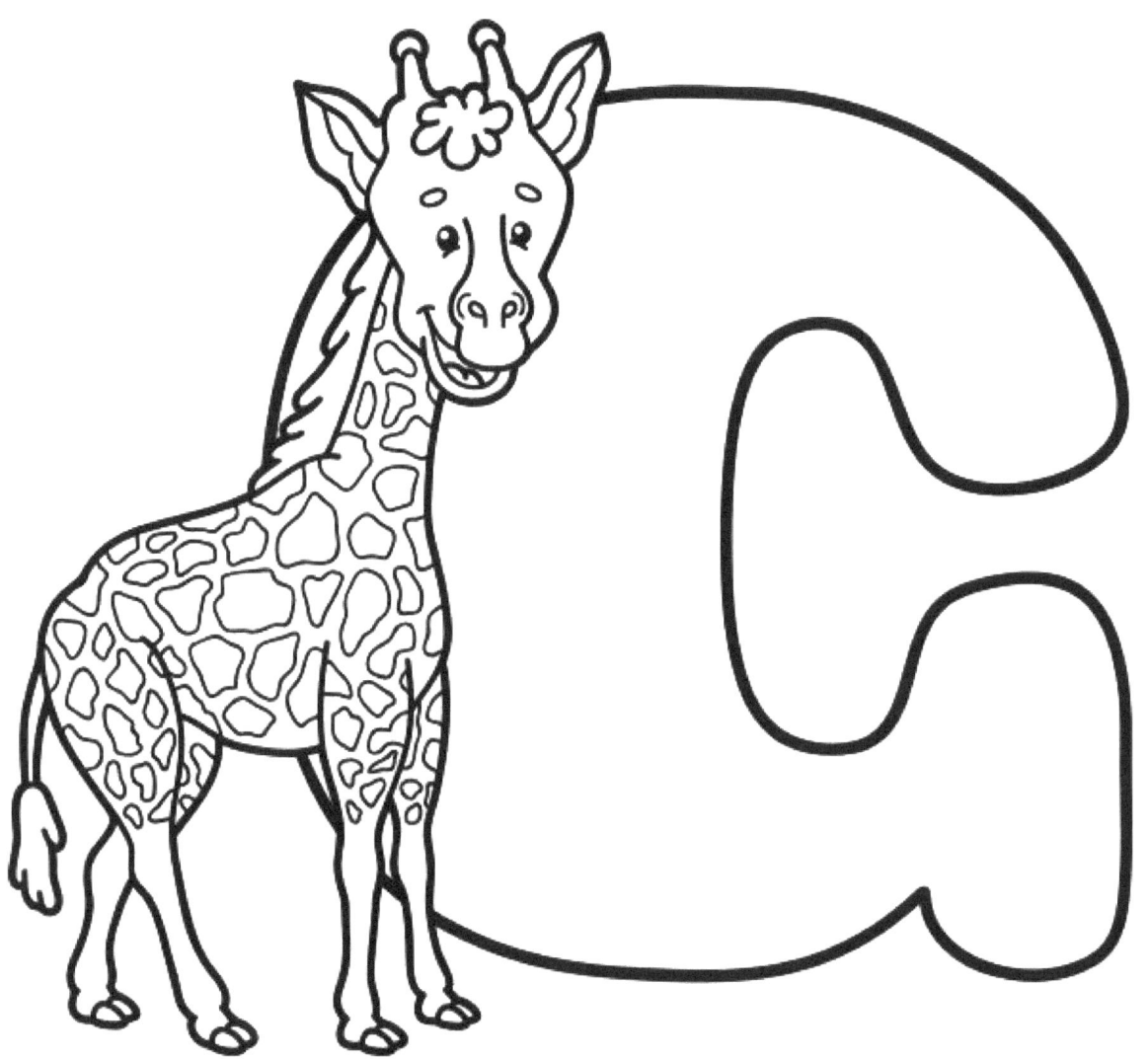

GIRAFFE

HEN

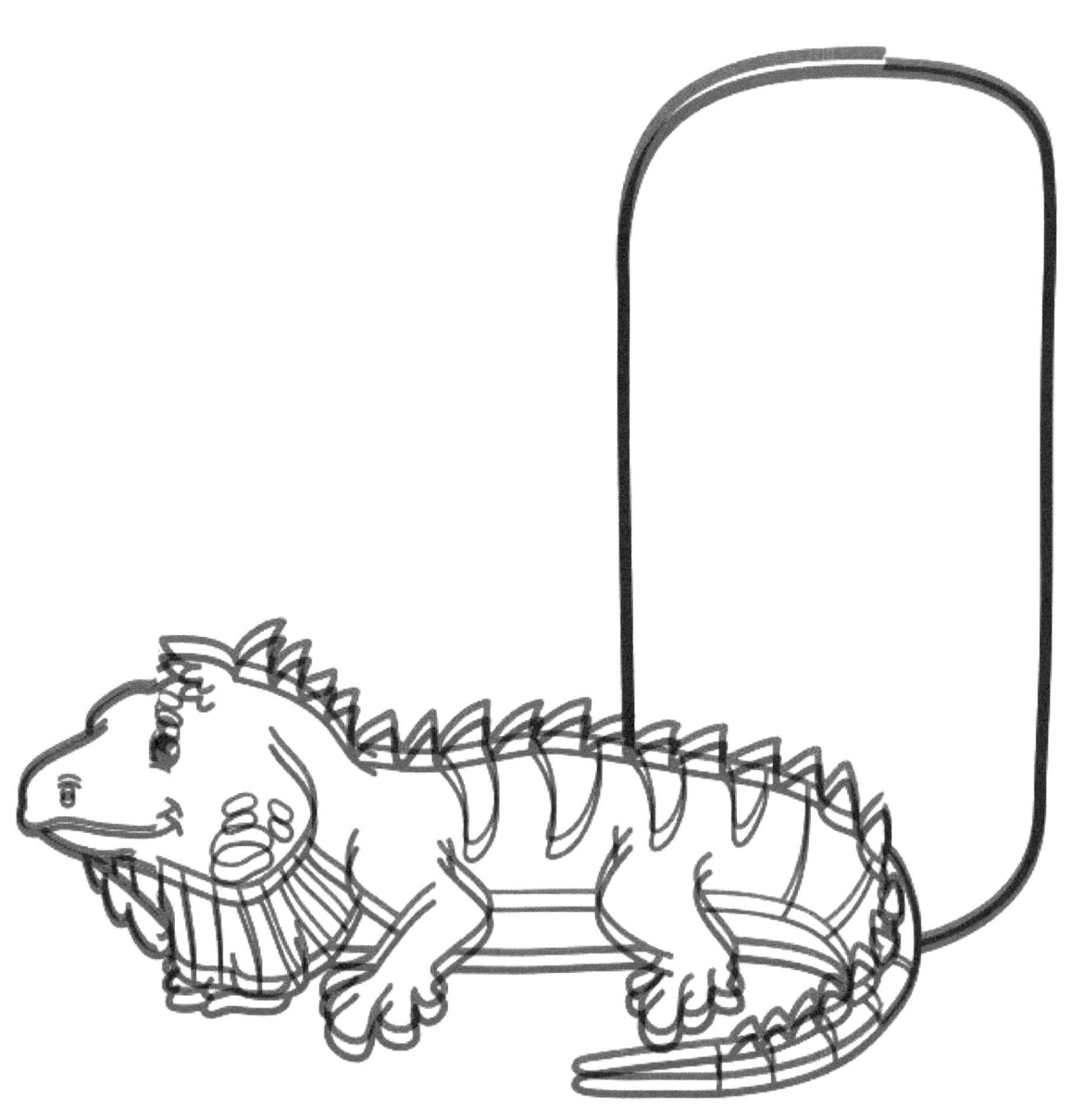
IGUANA

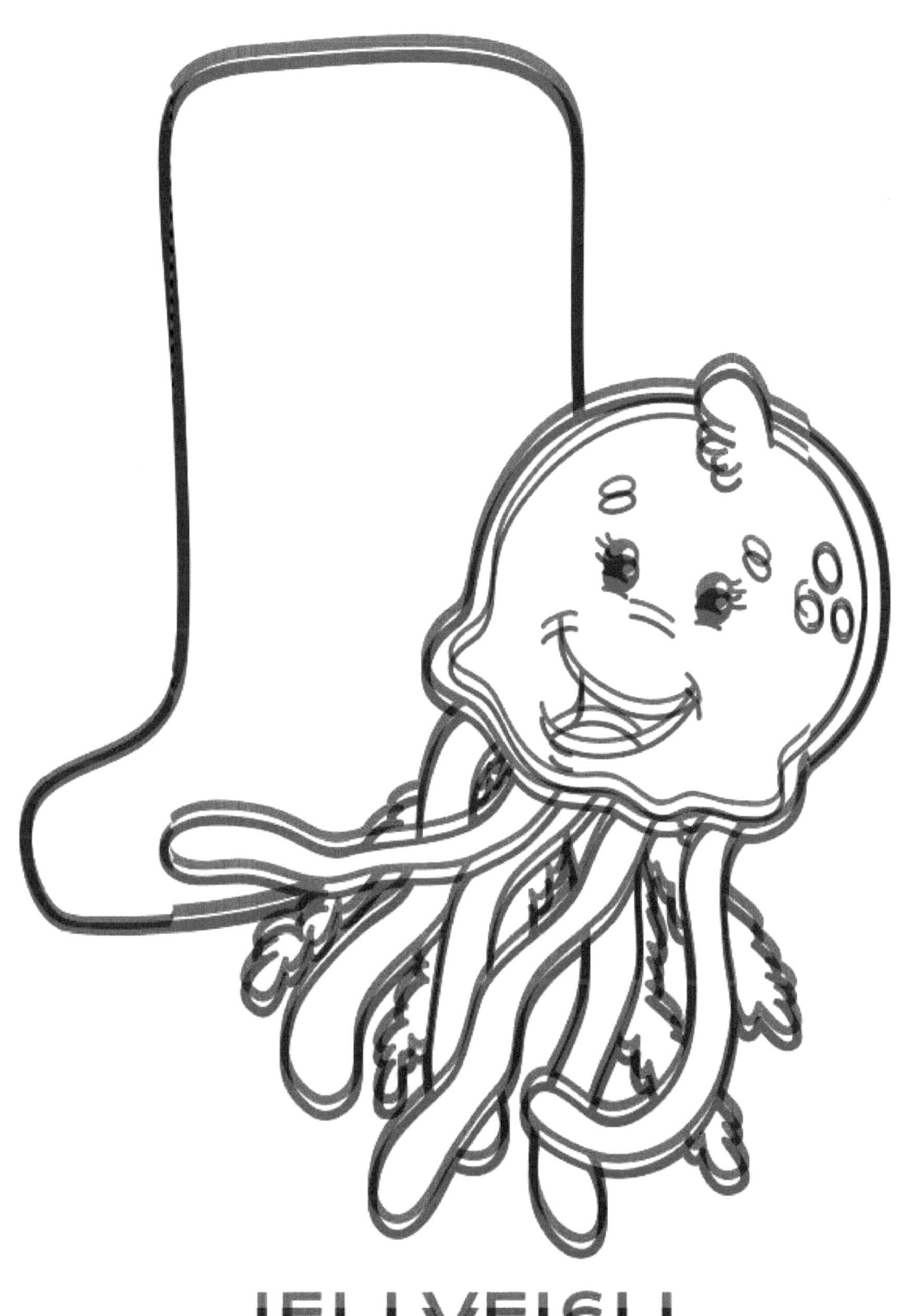

JELLYFISH

KOALA

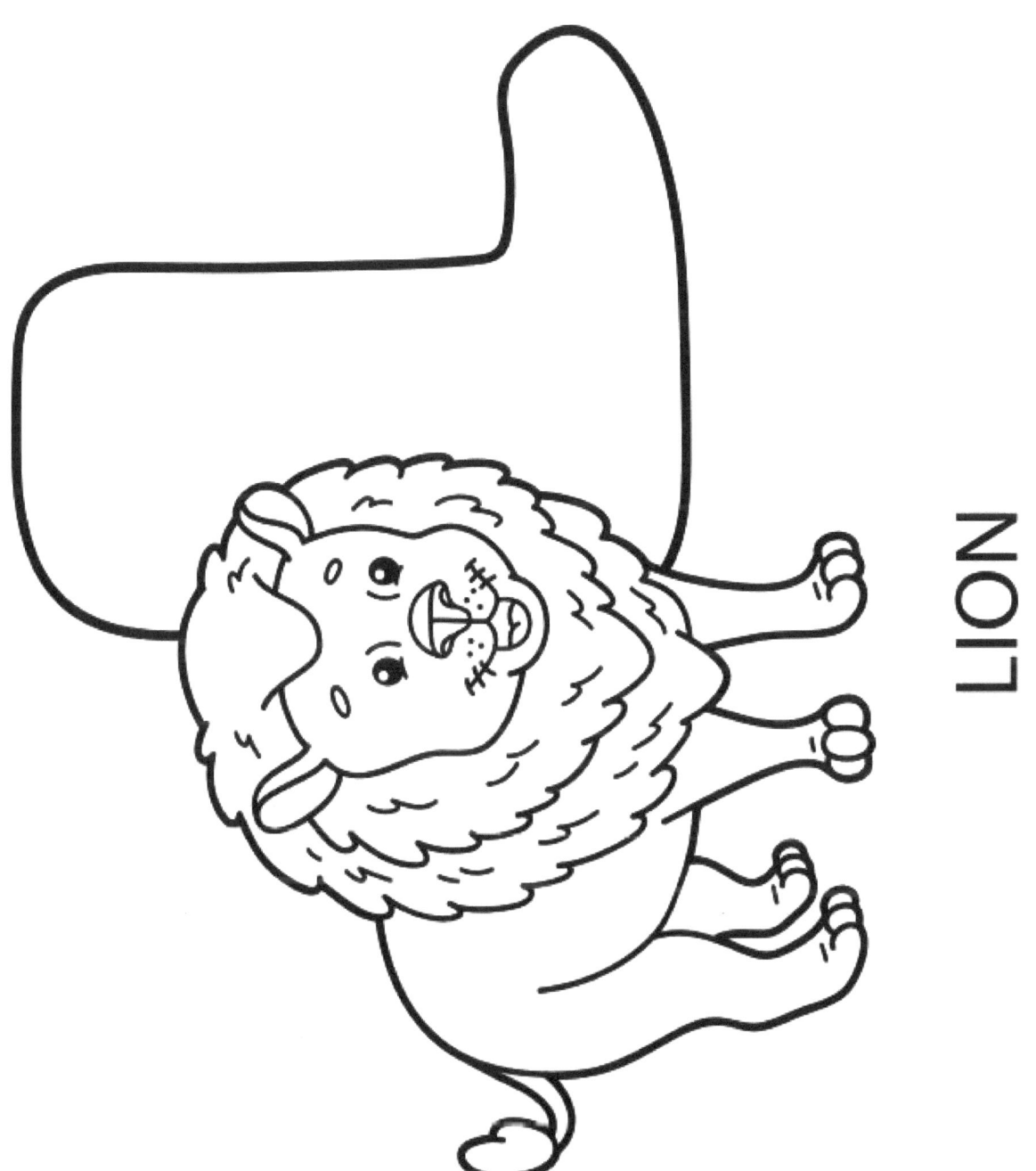

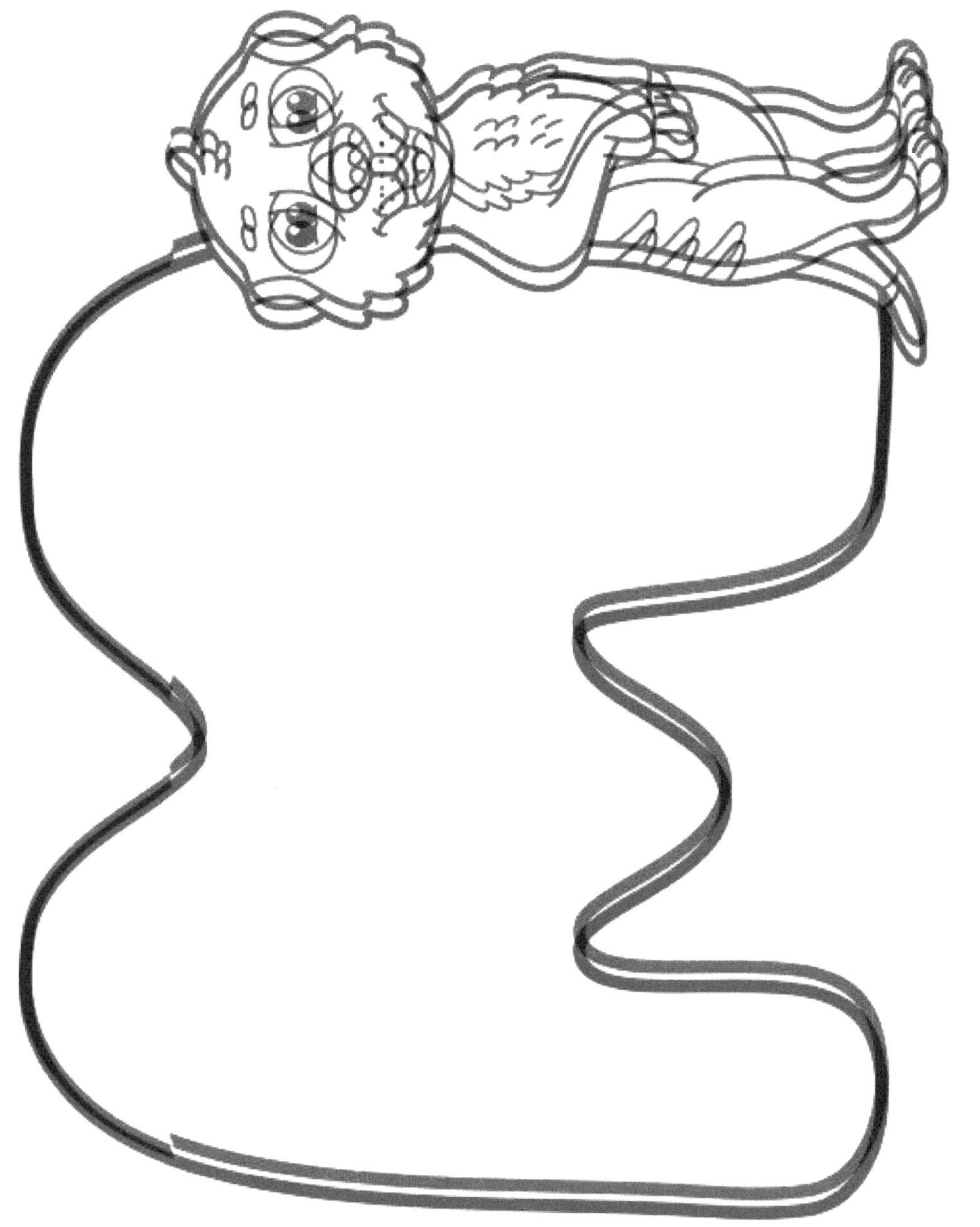

MEERKAT

NUMBAT

OSTRICH

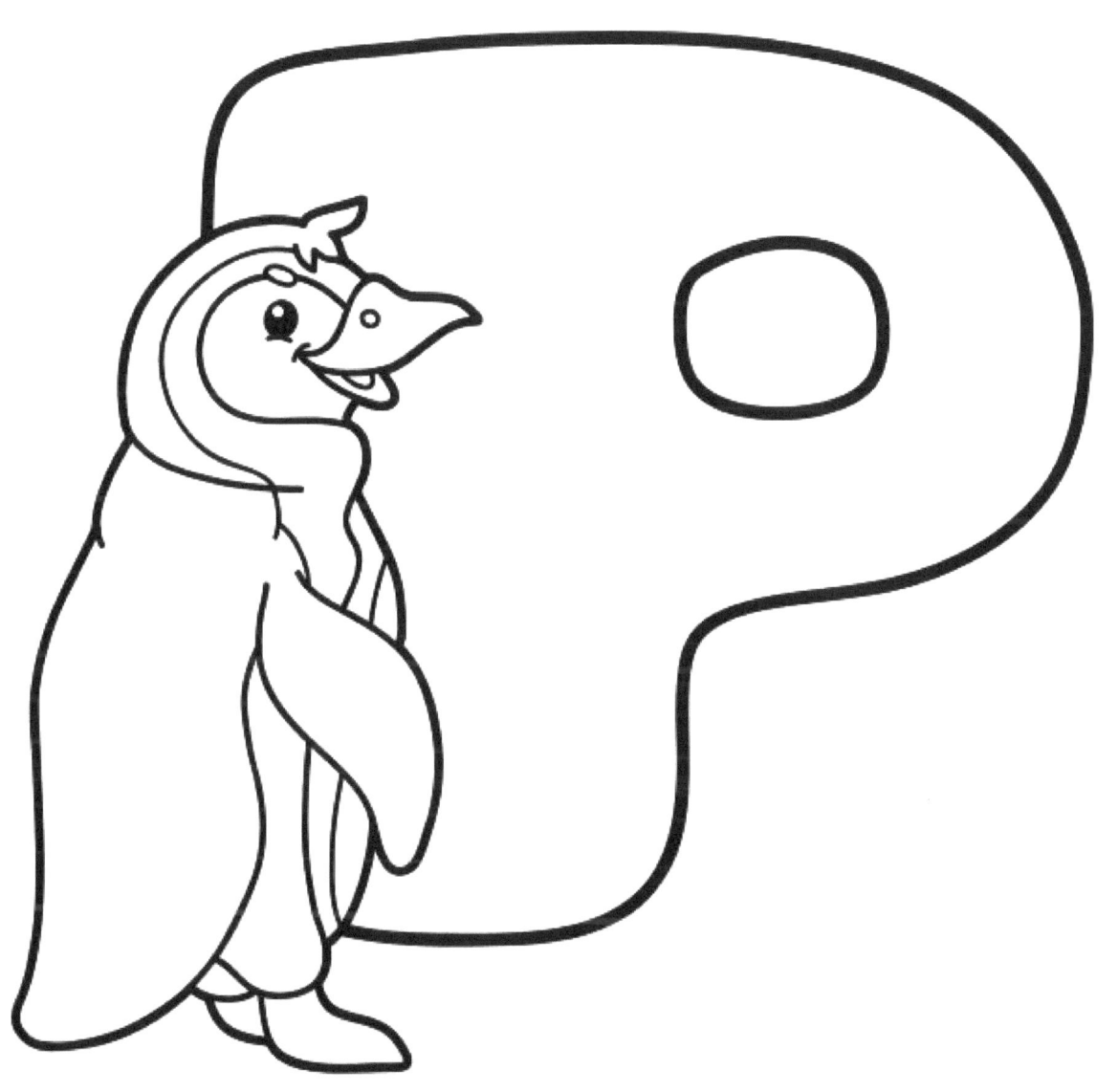

PENGUIN

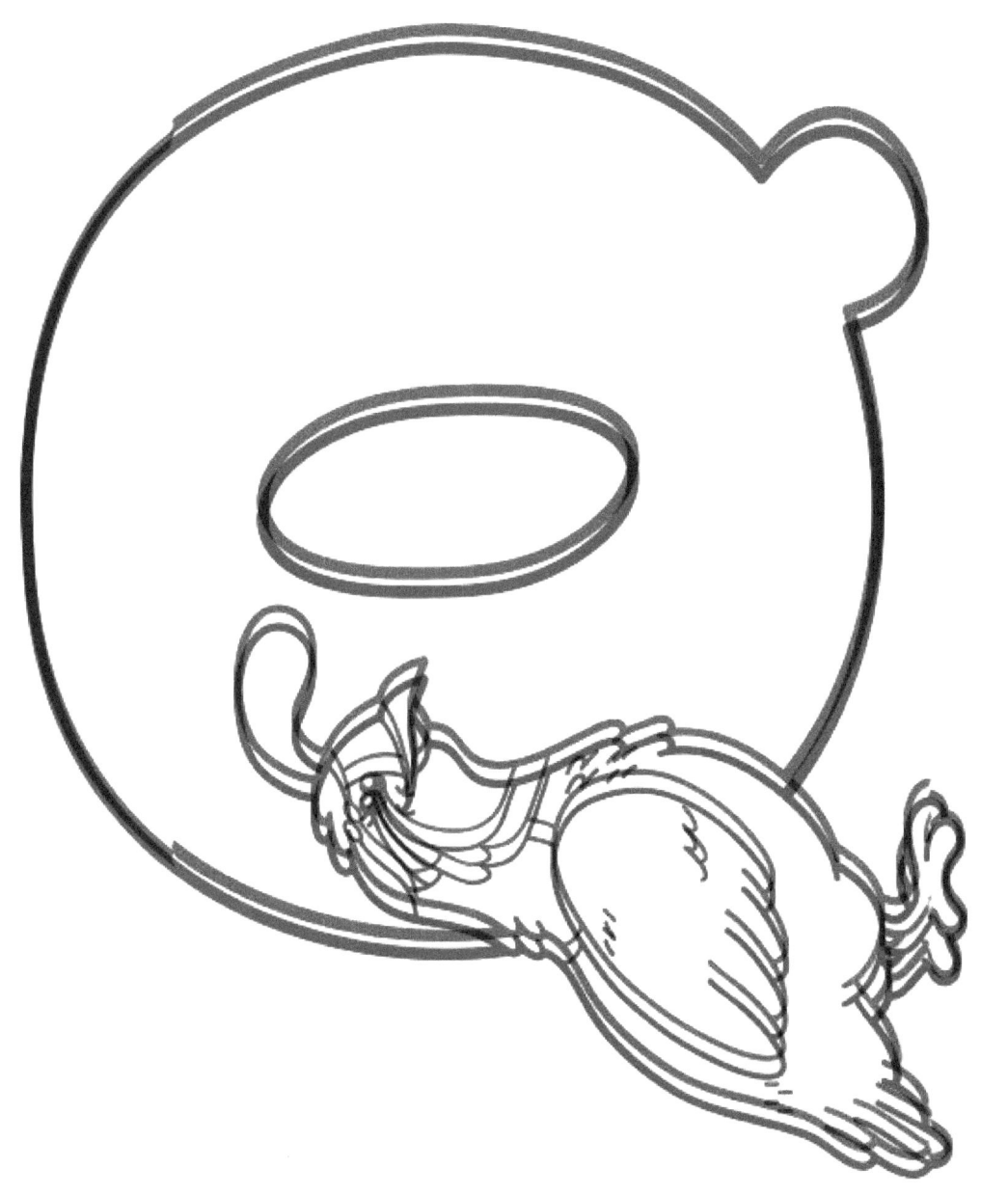

QUAIL

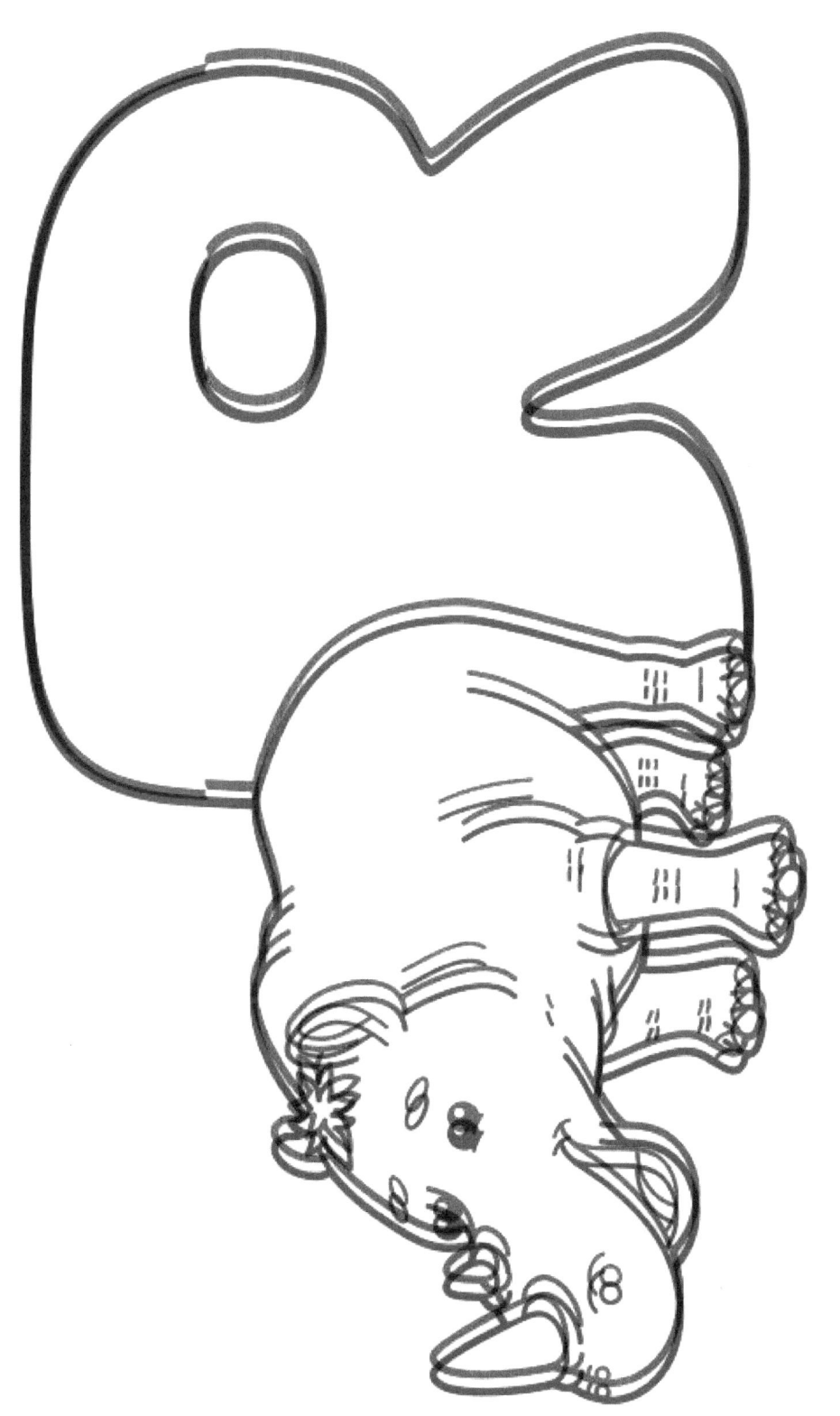

RHINO

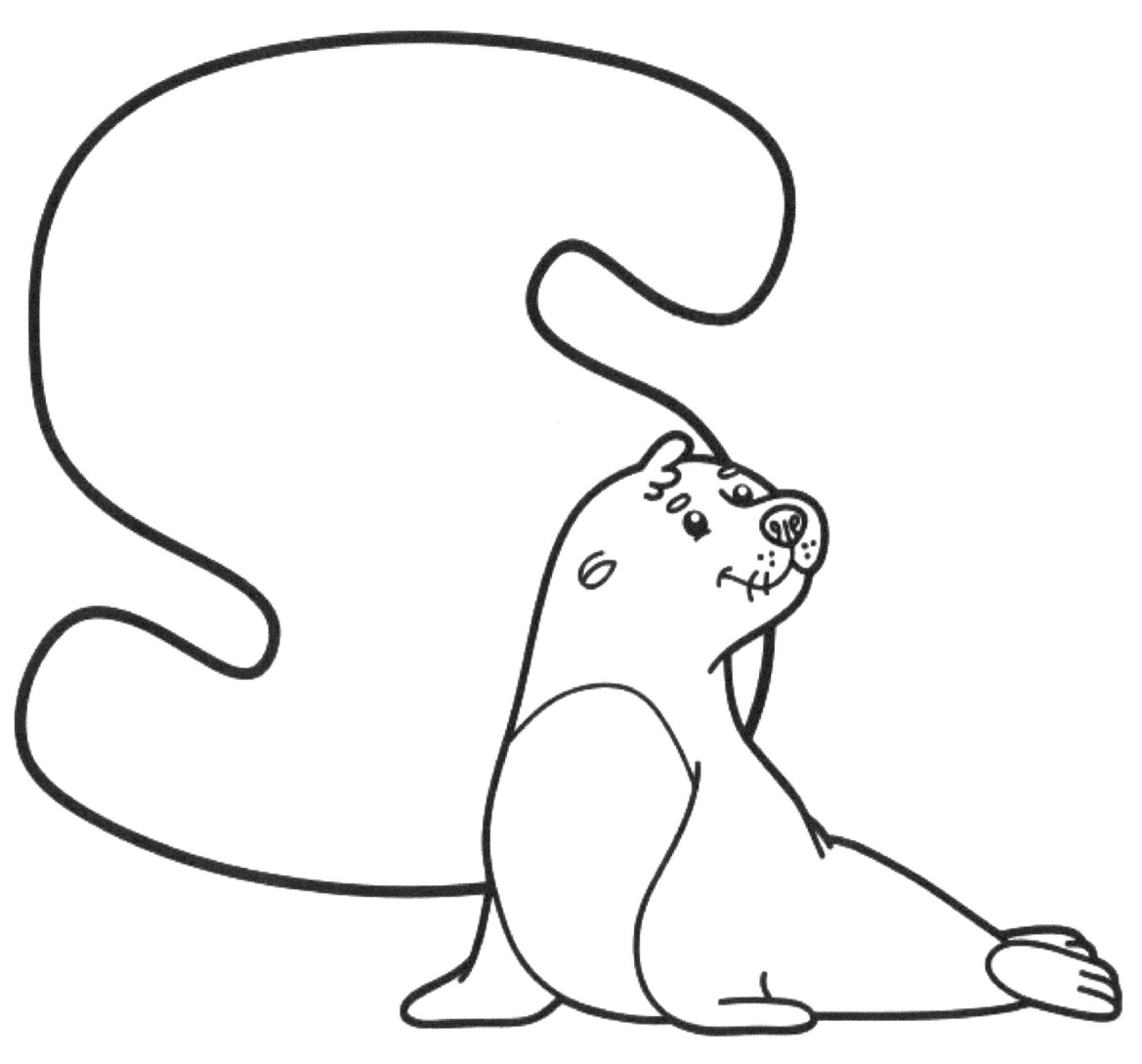

SEAL

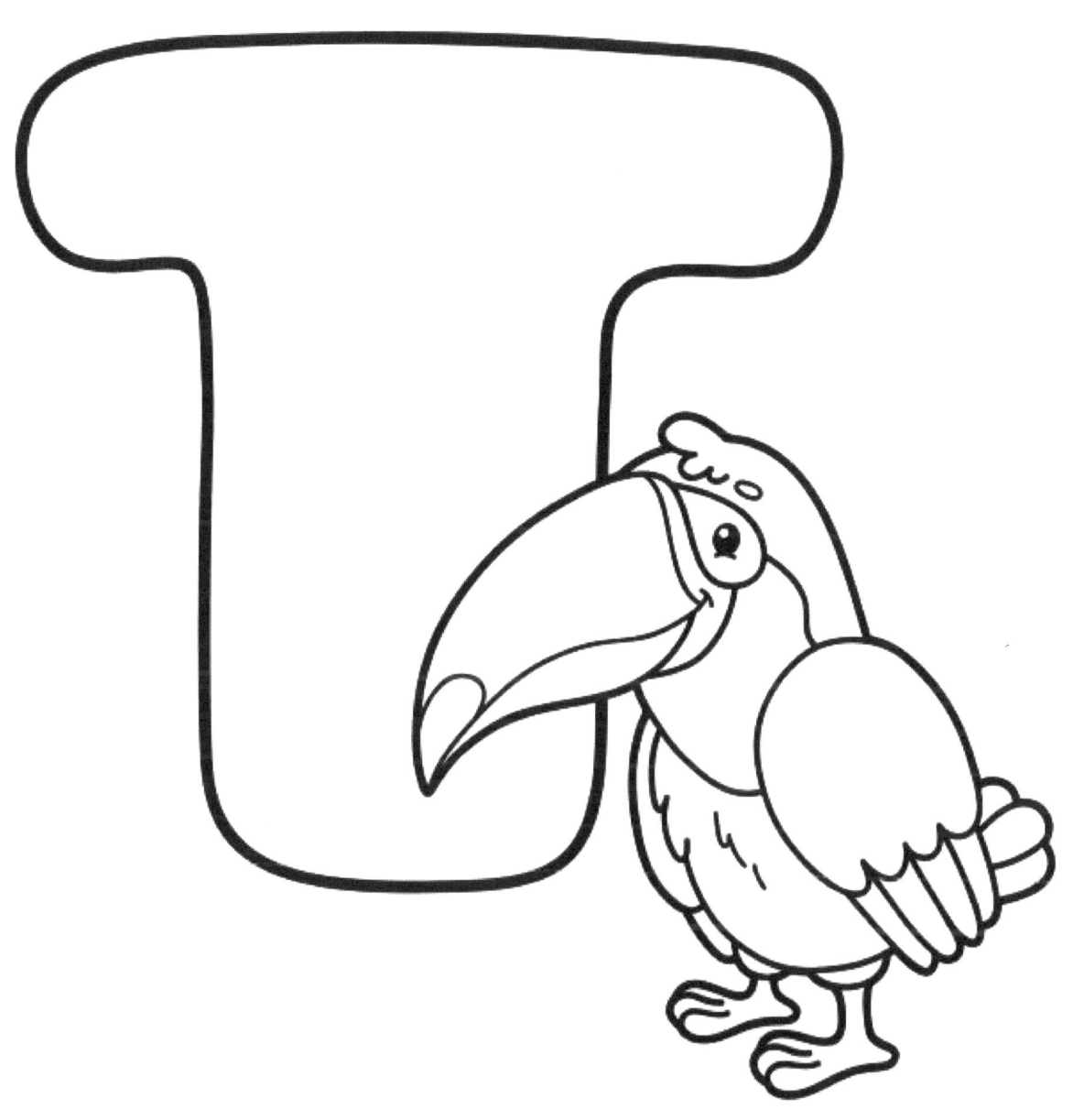

TOUCAN

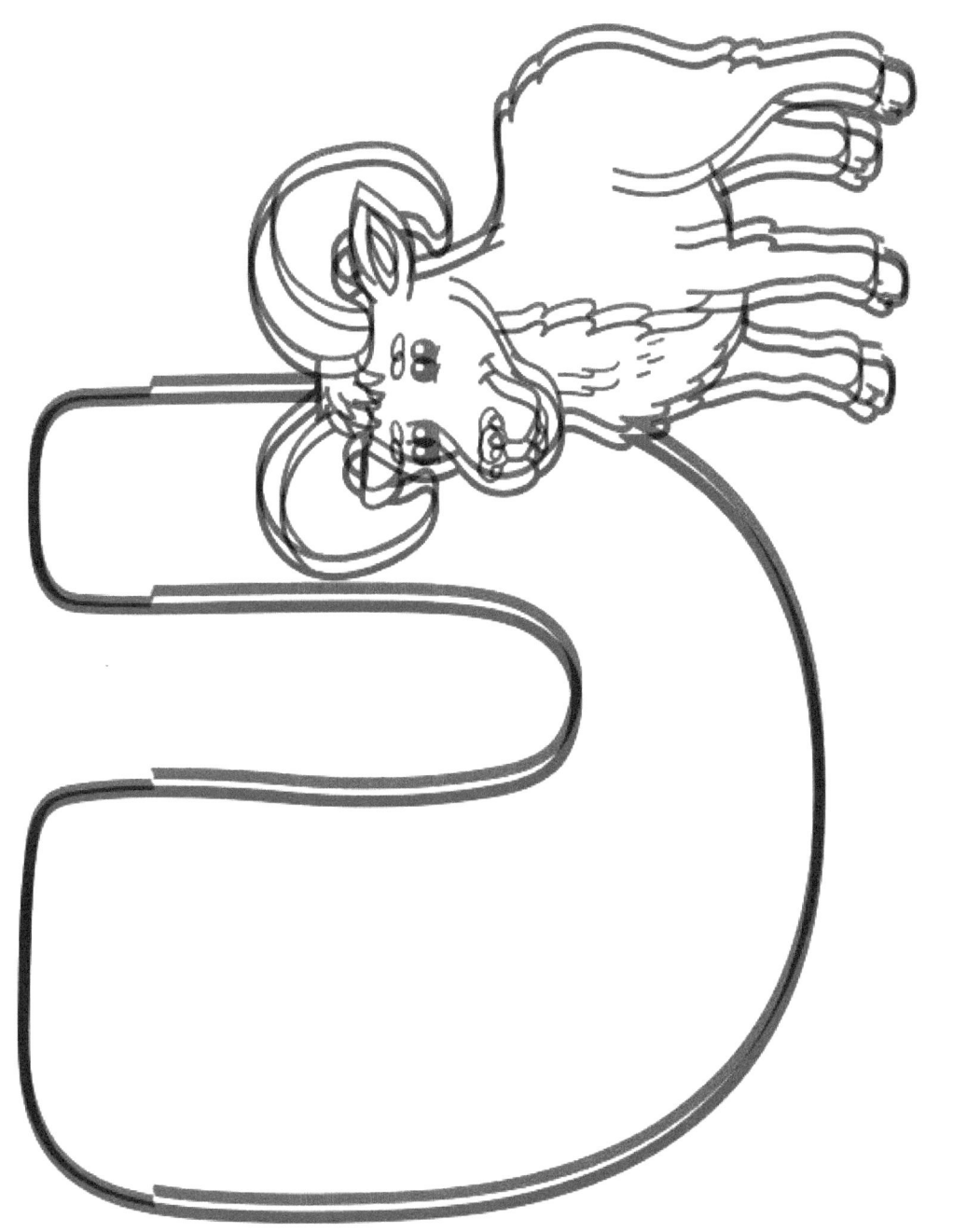

URIAL

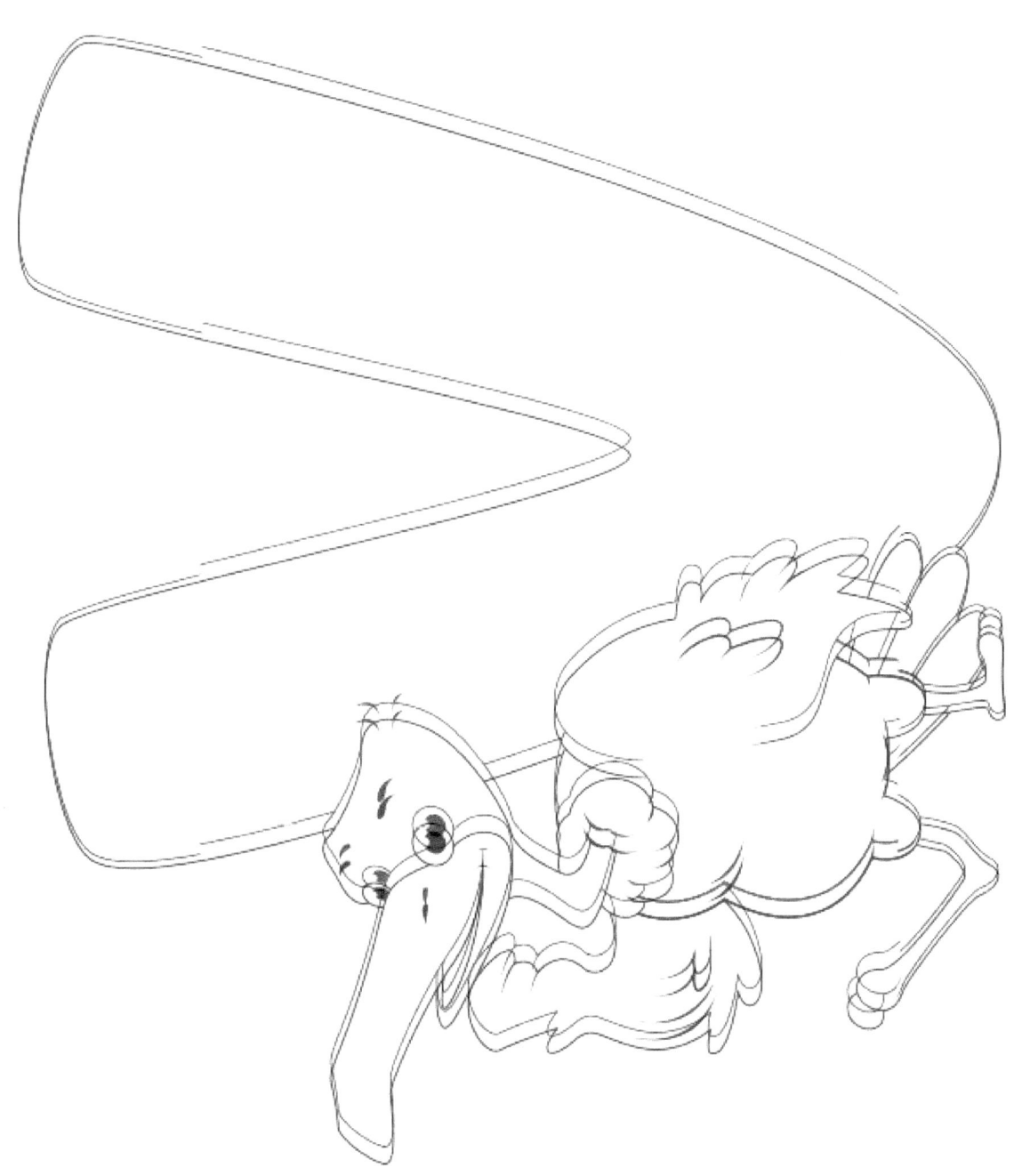

WHALE

XENOPS

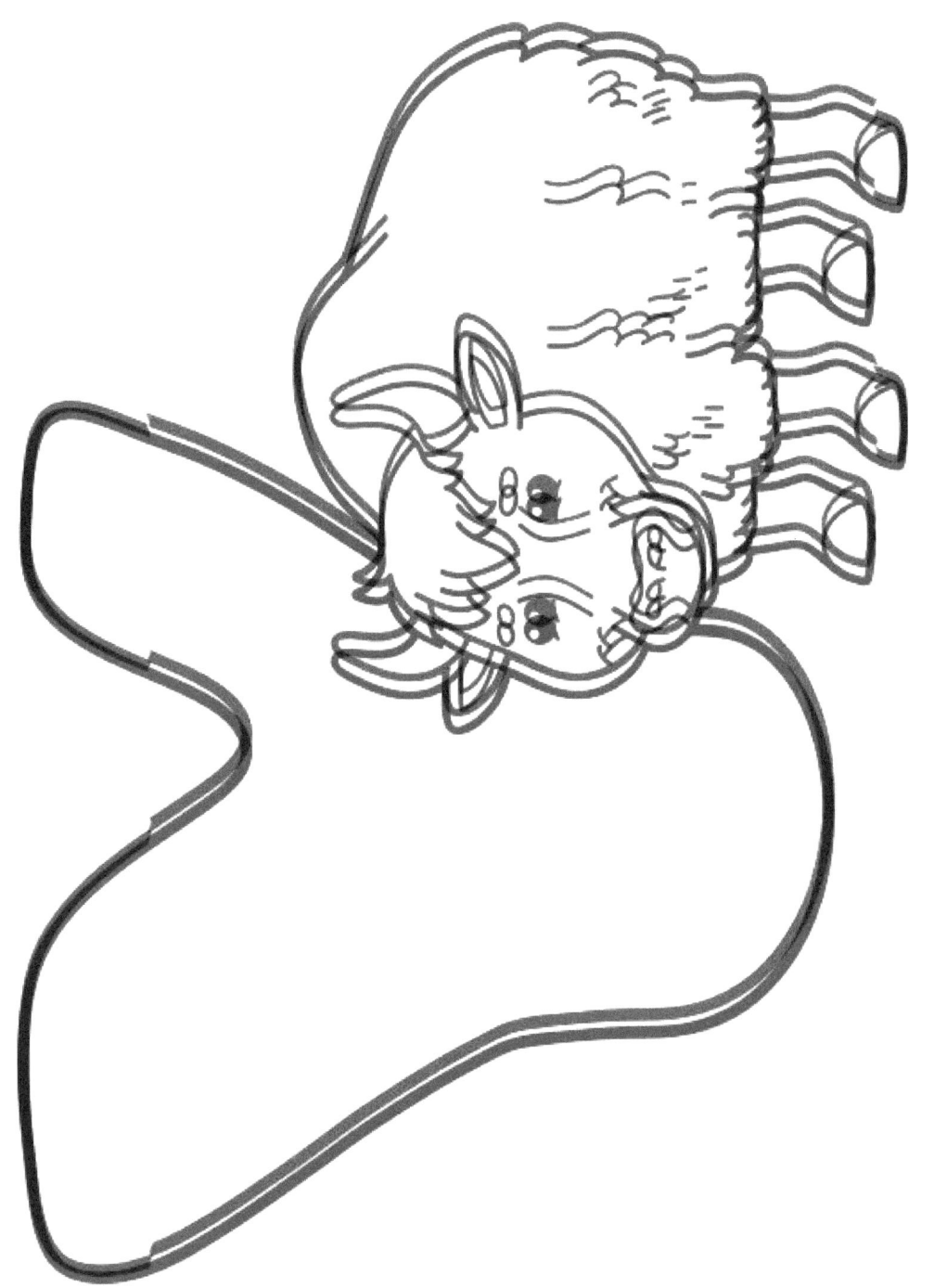

YAK

ZEBRA

BONUS

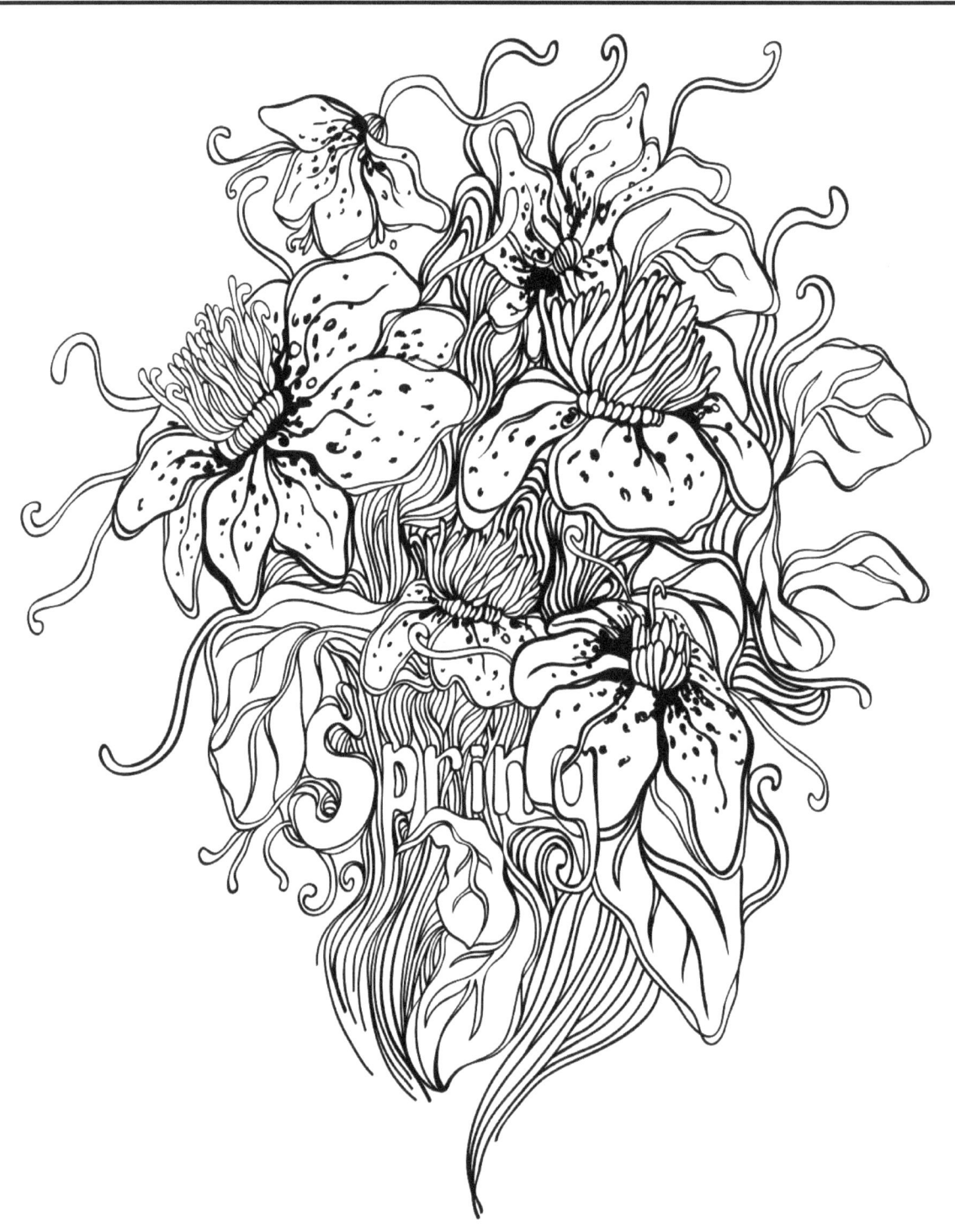

BONUS

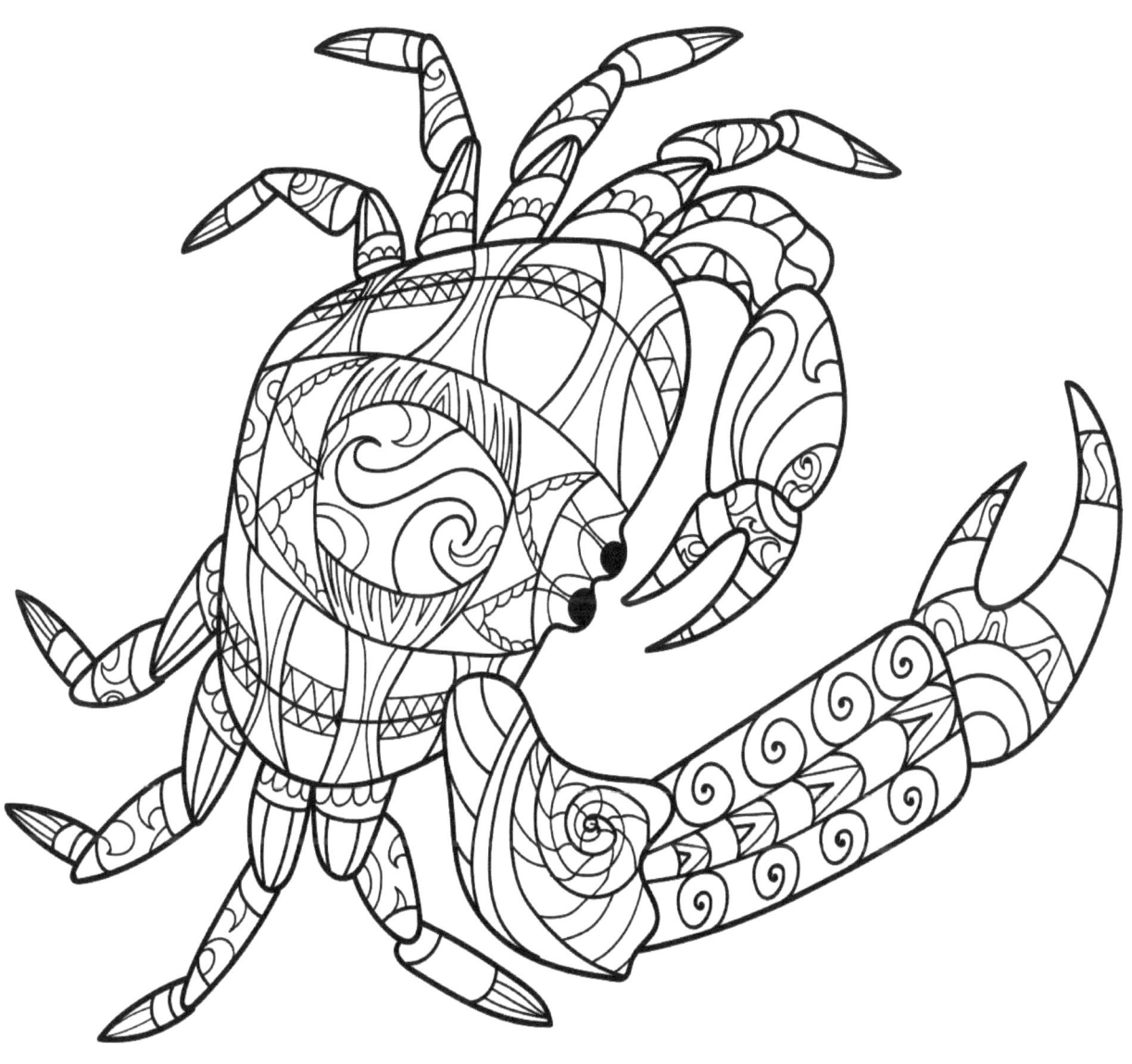

www.ingramcontent.com/pod-product-compliance
Lightning Source LLC
Chambersburg PA
CBHW051941210526

45473CB00006B/2338